Think Like It:
When Failure Is Not An Option

Michael E. Carter Jr.

Think Like It:
When Failure Is Not An Option

Michael E. Carter Jr.

ISBN ISBN-10: 0-692-97317-6
ISBN-13: 978-0-692-97317-2

Carter Development Systems LTD
1611 Arlington Ave.
Toledo, Ohio 43609

Dedication

I dedicate this book to my unbelievable wife and children. Tanika your trust and love is unmatched. You guys are the reason I wake up and pursue greatness relentlessly. This is one more step toward our collective legacies.

Isaiah Carter together we made magic. It may have cost us some pain along the way, but it was well worth it. The essence of this book is just as much about you as it is my journey.

Table of Contents

① *Start With the end in Mind*

*I*n this book, I am going to give you some proven secrets I have learned through trial and error, along with; some solid advice I have received from friends and colleagues over the years. I wish I had known these principles when I started because I could have accomplished much more in a shorter period of time. However, this book would probably be more of a college textbook, than the type of book that everyone with a desire to succeed would read.

Starting with a dream is important. Everyone can dream about where it is they want to be in ten, twenty, thirty years from now. Dreams are what make success possible for the average person. Let's think for a moment the chair that you sat in yesterday was someone else's dream. The car you drive is someone else's dream. This book that you are reading was a part of my dream. Everything in the world started out as a thought. The word Logos is a powerful word that baffles many scholars. The word could be used in a biblical sense to mean Word thus as you may notice from its capitalization it becomes a pronoun for God, or this word could merely mean interrelated thoughts. The reason why I point out the word logos is that it takes several interrelated thoughts to develop a sensible dream. What is a dream? The dictionary defines a dream as a series of thoughts not under the command of reason, to think; to imagine. Many people cannot remember the dreams that they have while they are asleep, but we all should remember dreams and aspirations that we carry close to our hearts.

I know you wonder why I decided to begin my book discussing dreams. Well, there are actually a couple of reasons. The first reason is the world likes to stereotype dreamers as people who never accomplish anything. They are just considered passionate. Secondly, because I believe the core basis to success in anything you set out to achieve begins with a dream. I have met with many cli ents in my office who want to give me the exciting details of a dream they recently had. The problem I find with most of the dreams is the person who had the dream does not know what to do with the dream or how to interpret it. Many of us have great ideas and inventions, but we do not know where to begin on our journey of fulfillment. Well, I learned that we must start with the end in mind.

Dreams are what make success possible for the average person

Let me explain what I mean. Whenever you have an idea, you are passionate about you should begin to put it in writing. You should write the vision and make it plain as Habakkuk said (Hab. 2:2). You must write every possible detail that you can think of that may be a necessary component to accomplishing success. Now sit down and write a summary of what it is you want to accomplish and how long you think it will take you. Now, you should write an outline from your ideas. Next, you should set goals that directly correspond to your idea. Make sure your goals are (S.M.A.R.T.) Strategic and Specific, Measurable, Attainable, Result-based, and Time-bound.[1] After you have done this ask yourself several questions, is my dream big enough? Does my dream seem impossible? If the answers are yes, then we are ready to begin your journey to greatness.

Whenever you have an idea, you are passionate about you should begin to put it in writing

When your dream seems to be bigger than life it challenges you to become focused. In Gary Keller's book "The Millionaire Real Estate Agent," he talks about aiming to Climb Mount Everest. By setting your goals to climb Mount Everest, you will be able to climb all the smaller mountains in between where you are and your goal.[2] The point that I am trying to make is that you should not aim

---

[1] Anne Conzemius and Jan O'Neill, The Power of SMART Goals: Using Goals to Improve Learning (Bloomington, IN,: Solution Tree Press, 2006), 13.
[2] Gary Keller and Dave Jenks, The Millionaire Real Estate Agent: It's Not About the Money… It's About Being the Best You Can Be! (NY: McGraw-Hill, 2004), 124.

too low. Shoot for the stars and hit the moon. Set your goals high enough that you always have something pushing you. Your goals will cause you to develop an optimistic attitude oppose to a negative one. In fact, you will still feel like there is more that can be accomplished.

Here is the great thing about starting with the end in mind. You will always have a clear road map of where it is that you are going to end up. You will take all the guesswork out and avoid the trap of depression in the difficult times of life. This will also keep you from feeling like you do not have a sense of direction while trying to climb the ladder of success. When you ask others for help, they will all ask you the same question. That question is where are you going and why? Now because we started with the end in mind, you will have a crystal clear answer for them.

Watch the end of the movie first for a change

The next time you buy a movie fast forward to the end and watch that first. In fact, you probably have noticed many movie writers are known for starting their movies from the end and working backward. This technique changes how you view the events of the movie. I have learned this technique causes you to pay closer attention to the intrinsic details of the movie. It is amazing that this also works in life. When you understand what the success of your goals looks like you will be able to define all the necessary steps to achieve your desired outcome. Success is not rocket science or brain surgery in fact success is a byproduct of discipline.

I know you think watching the end of the movie first makes absolutely no sense at all, but it actually does. Watching the end of the movie also tells you who the key people are in the movie. This is a management ingredient that I am sharing with you now. High achievers and successful managers both know how to identify who are the key people to their success. By outlining your vision and knowing the end from the beginning, you will not find yourself being hindered by people who are yellow lights on your road to success.

A successful screenwriter will keep you on the edge of your seat even if you already know the end of the movie. The end of the movie shows you the outcome but fails to give you details concerning its arrival. Details are an essential ingredient to success. Every character present at the end of the movie may not have been in the beginning, so the plot is vital to defining their roles. It is the same way with relationships in the life of successful leaders. They know what type of person will help them reach their goals they just do not know where they will meet them in life.

The last thing about watching the end of the movie first is that it will cause you to paint a picture in your mind about how everything ends up. All the screen magic in the world will not be able to erase what you already know to be true. I really believe this is how life is meant to be. That no matter what happens to you on a daily basis you should keep a clear picture in your mind about how everything you desire is supposed to end up. The long hours of hard work, research, and studying will not seem to be so long when you know you are inching closer to success. This simple technique may prove to be one of the most valuable practices that you will ever have. Life hands you many challenges and obstacles, but we must employ every tactic that we can to overcome those struggles.

The finish line looks the same

When I played football in high school, our coach required us to run a mile every day in our team sports class. Let me start by saying this seems to be an impossible task for a freshman who has never run any further than he had to. To make matters worse many of the people in the class had never run a mile before either. In all our other drills, we were told to run has hard and fast as we could. So, when I was trying to figure out how was I going to have the strength to run a mile faster than anyone else on the track the task became staggering to my mind. Oh, yeah there is one more thing I should mention about this, and that is that the track was old and on the second level of the gym. Every time anyone would run on this track it felt as if the track would fall. Here is where I learned my first lesson about not looking down

Life hands you many challenges and obstacles, but we must employ every tactic that we can to overcome those struggles

but always staying focused. You must not worry about where you are now, but you must remember what your destiny is. Here I am at the front of the line waiting for the coach to blow the whistle so I could begin this journey of running a mile. However, I still had one problem I did not know where the finish line was but, before I could ask, the coach blew the whistle, and we all took off. After my first time around the track, I asked the coach where was the finish line. His reply was right where you started. Amazing! I found out that the end of the mile was the same place where I started the only difference was the amount of times I traveled the same path.

The lesson that I learned that day was one of the greatest lessons of the rest of my life. You see every time we end one task we are beginning another. I prefer to begin my entire task with the end in mind. I learned that as long as I did not look down, I did not have a fear of falling. I also learned that life is not a sprint to the end rather a journey we must all follow. Life is not a race where I must be the first to the finish line because success is measured on progress not speed. Do more every day than you did the day before and perfect your skills, talents, and gifts so that you become the best person available for the task not the first person in the door. Being a realtor taught me that it is not the person with the first appointment but the person that was most prepared that gets the deal.

The finish line should not be your goal. When you are a high achiever, you are not just looking to finish you are looking to maximize your opportunities. Your goals should only get larger as you go on they should never stop existing. Before reaching your current goals make sure to set new ones. A person who does not set goals is a person who is willing to settle for being average. In fact, when you stop dreaming you stop living. Your dreams are

Leadership Alert: Sharpening your skills will push you through your limits doorways of tomorrow. A finish line is just a place where you look to see how far away success really is.

It takes all the stress away

Everyone can defuse stress when you begin to feel overwhelmed. However, you are more likely to become stressed out when you are not sure how you are going to succeed at any given task. This comes mostly from a lack of preparation. There could be many reasons why you feel as if you are not prepared, beginning with not fully comprehending the assignment you were given. I view every task, goal, or business transaction as an assigment that life has given me. I make it a habit not to rush, but I pride myself on being efficient, reliable, and aggressive on every assignment. When you know what the objective of the assingment is and understand that you are qualified to accomplish it, stress will not be able to overtake you. Preparation will allow you to be calm in the midst of adversity. By starting with the end in mind, you are telling the world that I can accomplish great things because I am prepared to weather the storm.

A prepared person is ready for most things that life throws their way. This is a person who keeps a toolkit in the trunk of their car because *A person who does* you never know when you may *not set goals is a* have an unplanned incident *person who is* with your car. Is not this the rea- *willing to settle for* son why we should have a spare *being average* tire in our cars? Think of it this way by having a spare tire I am not made immobile while I wait for others to carry me to my destination. The spare tire actually empowers me to reach my destination even if I hit a pothole that could stop my progress. I want you to remember that person who has prepared can never be stopped. If you are prepared for success, you will not have to wait for a person to help you who may be jealous or envious of your progress.

Nervous energy can sometimes become positive energy but not very often. When you are nervous, you will often forget to pay close attention to details and other things that seem mundane. I have also found that it is challenging to stay focus when I am nervous. Practice and preparation allow me to forecast future events and success. Preparation will propel you to expected heights of success. I set aside time every day for preparation and organization. Make sure that while you are planning your schedule that you schedule time for planning.

It is a wonderful feeling when you have prepared to become successful because you know that there is nothing that can stop you from reaching your destiny. Your hard work will pay off, and finally, your abilities will shine. This is the way you should feel every day. A prepared day is a stress-free day. When you are prepared to face adversity, you will not be stressed out about becoming a high achiever because you cannot do anything but be successful.

Count sheep or count backward

This will be my last point about starting with the end in mind. I do not want to overemphasize the point, but I want to make sure you understand the importance of this fundamental principle. I want you to think for a moment on those late nights when your parents made you go to sleep when you were not ready. Your parents may have told you to count sheep or to count backward. Maybe it was your dentist who told you to do this after he gave anesthesia before he performed open mouth surgery on you. Never the less, the point here is that you were given a direction to do something different than what was considered normal for you. The task may have even seemed awkward to you at first but not impossible. The interesting point here is the reason why the task does not feel impossible. It does not feel impossible to you because you already know all the numbers. You understand that you can take your time and think your way through the order of the numbers. You also realize that you can start over if you need to. Notice how by starting at the end you have taken all the pressure and stress away because to start at the end of a thing you must already understand the principles of the beginning of that very thing.

The funny thing is that most people never actually

finish counting backward. The same is true with counting sheep. We usually just give up, get tired of counting, or simply fall asleep. It is human nature, to simply give up on a task that seems impossible, or that may not have an exact end in sight like counting sheep. When you are told to count sheep or to count backward, you do not have to think about the reason why you are completing this task. The same must become true with your goals. Set your goals and follow your plan. Your plan should become a system that you follow to reach your goals. You should come to the point where you do not even think about it as a chore to do anymore. Once I started following a system I learned I could do more things in one day than I ever could before. The best part is that my system feels natural to me now. The hard task has now become doable be-cause I know what the end is expected to be.

② *Big Dreams Need Big Models*

$\mathcal{N}$ow let's take time and begin looking deep into your dreams again. Must we reexamine our initial question of is your dream big enough? Take your time and turn your dream into a vision. When you can turn your dream into a vision, it will take on a life of its own. It will be able to outlive you and future generations. After you leave this life, your vision becomes a testament of who you are for all to benefit. You can achieve great things so dare to dream more than you have ever imagined before. You will be successful so enlarge that dream beyond your wildest imagination. Kick your faith into high gear and, like Jabez, ask God to enlarge your territory (1 Chron. 4:10).

Listen, do not ask anybody if your dream makes sense because if it does make sense to them than you need to dream some more. Your dream should seem unachievable to other people. It should leave them wondering if such a thing is even possible. Let me share this with you, Bishop Oscar Hayes of Detroit, Michigan once said this at a conference I was hosting, "If you can think it you can have it" that is a powerful statement. I started reflecting on the bishop's words, and it began to make

13

perfectly good sense to me, if I can comprehend it then I can achieve it. Wow! What a concept. Do you realize the power that you just equipped yourself with by reading that statement? That means that any dream that you begin to visualize you can achieve it. Let's slow down before we go too far and review what we have learned up to this point.

1. Dream It
2. Write It
3. Summarize It
4. Outline It
5. Believe It
6. Set Goals That Are S.M.A.R.T.

Now that we have our big dreams in place let's begin to develop our initial plans. There are a few more questions that we must start to ask ourselves to birth something fruitful. These questions are whom we have seen do this before? What does this most resemble? Am I

If I can comprehend it then I can achieve it

passionate about it? Who will ever care that I did it? The answers to these questions are significant. The first response should sound something like this, well no one has done it quite the way I am trying to. The next answer will vary based on the dream; however, the last two have an incredibly personalized answer which should sound something like this yes I am passionate about it, and all the people who benefit from my success will care that I did it? Hopefully, you are beginning to realize your dreams will benefit allow those whom it touches.

Start with this thought in mind, "Whose idea is it." This thought will remind you that this is your dream and it is up to you to chart its course. I have a belief that when I am sleeping and my dreams turn into nightmares that I can turn them back into peaceful dreams. I know that I can cause things to happen in my dreams. This concept helps me frame the dreams for my life in the real world. I understand that I can control the outcomes in my life by meditation, prayer, and perseverance. Nothing is too hard for me to face or handle. Develop a proven model for your dream and stick to it no matter what happens. Your dreams need big models to be put in place in order to have room to grow the way you intend. When you have a model in place, you can predetermine the expansion and growth of your vision. Keep in mind that the model you chose is the framework for birthing your dream.

Where are you going?

After you have put the final touches on your dream, you must write it into a summary. It is at this point that your dream becomes a vision. If your idea remains a dream, it is not ready for use. Think of your dream in comparison of the first two trimesters of pregnancy for an expecting mom. You know the baby is not prepared to live on its own if delivered now, so it is with your dream as well. Once you summarize your dream, you have given it a body for which it can live. Your summary is what other people can comprehend and begin to gain some insight into what it is you are trying to accomplish. Your summary will make it easier for you to write your outline but do not let guru's read this because they think they have a better way.

If your idea remains a dream, it is not ready for use

Your outline is your roadmap to success. It is your outline that you will refer to every time you make a personal or business decision that can affect the rest of your life. I am sure you have heard the saying always follow your first mind, well your first thought is your outline. In fact, we call your outline the key elements of your plan. I know that there is a stereotype out there that says if a man is lost he will not ask for directions well I do not follow that school of philosophy. I ask for directions before I ever leave home. I do not want to be lost. I do not like the dreadful feeling that it gives me, as well as it is the breeding ground for arguments. If you want to destroy great times on a trip just get lost, not only does the driver get frustrated but everyone who is in the car picks up a negative attitude. Our lives are the same way. Many of us live our lives without any clear directions, lost on the road of achievement not knowing what it is we are going to accomplish. This is why many marriages fail, and families are destroyed. It is also the reasons for low morale in a company or the lack of excitement in the launching of a new church initiative. Always keep your roadmap close to you because it may be the very thing that keeps your dream alive.

Before I go any further, I do not want to make any assumptions about you as a reader. I want you to achieve great things in life. I want you to be the best at whatever you are endeavoring to do. You do not end up successful by chance or circumstance. Success is achieved because of discipline and hard work. By discipline, I mean doing those things which are productive on a continual basis. You need to have a system which enables you to determine if you are successful. One small helpful idea would be to use your planner regularly. You do not have to buy a major brand name because that is what everyone else has. Go to your local office supply store and look at all the styles that are available and pick one that you are comfortable with at a price you can afford. A simple planner with a "to do list" can help you organize your day. Smartphones, tablet, and iPads are useful as well, but they also run the risk of becoming major distractions. Gadgets and technology have pros and cons that you have to measure your ability to be productive. It is also essential to prepare a backup plan if you lose the device.

Every night before you go to sleep you should write down the five things you must do the next morning before you do anything else. Start focusing on the must do's we all have them, but we do not all do them when we are supposed to. I had to stop and point to this aspect of preparation just to make sure that organization stays at the forefront of your mind. Many people think that if they are not in corporate America, they do not need a planner or calendar. Well, I am going to let the secret out of the bag we are all in corporate America in one way or another. You are either a statistic of corporate America or a component of someone else's success in Corporate America. That great American Rapper Jay Z said it best when he uttered the phrase, "I am not a businessman, I am a business, man."[1] If you are not currently living an organized life, make organization your first goal. Make it a priority because you are a business, brand, and walking billboard.

You must know where you are headed. Having a clear understanding of your goals will mean you have a clear understanding of your objective. Clarity should

---

[1] Kanye West and Jay Z, Diamonds from Sierra Leone: Remix (Produced by Kanye West, Devo Springsteen, and Jon Brion)

be more than a buzzword in your life. If you want to be successful, you will need a clear path to get there. Your dreams, visions, plans, and goals will follow a different process than other people. Writing your five must-do task the night before will cause you to become more intentional about where you burn your energy daily. Precision in preparation elevates you above those who are willing to settle for average results. Plan your daily activities because your to-do list becomes the directions on your map of success.

I-75

One day while traveling down I-75 in Michigan headed to Toledo, Ohio I ran into construction. I had a speaking engagement at four o'clock pm, and it was already twenty minutes after three, and I still had about a forty-minute drive without construction. I saw that I was going to have a problem when I noticed that all the traffic came to a complete stop. As I looked further ahead, I could see a yellow arrow flashing forcing all the cars into one lane. I immediately turned my radio onto one of the local news stations to hear about possible construction detour routes

Precision in preparation elevates you above those who are willing to settle for average results

only to hear the highway was closed near my destination. I had no idea what to do since I was going to a city where I was not familiar with its roads and highway systems. I did not have a map because except for a few turns I have traveled this path before. What I had to do was think of where it was I was trying to end up. I remember seeing Telegraph road on a previous trip to Toledo. Therefore, I knew if I just made a few adjustments to my path, I could find my way to telegraph and navigate to my engagement from there.

If you start with the end in mind, you will be able to overcome any obstacles. I later learned that Interstate 75 could take me all the way to Florida from Michigan. That was interesting to me because if I can follow the interstate signs, I could make the drive and not get lost. There may be construction and even closed roads on my path, but the detours should not block me from reaching my destination. In life, we all face adversity and challenges. These challenges may delay you, but they should not stop you from reaching your destiny. Be confident that you are moving down the road of success as you navigate through your plans.

Confidence is an essential ingredient to success. A person who is empowered is confident about their ability to be successful. Why do you ask? Well, because someone had to give you the power to be confident by trusting you to be responsible or to complete a specific task. Just as I had to navigate my way down I-75 by using landmarks that were familiar to me, a high achiever must recognize landmarks on the road to success. These landmarks are what I like to call goals. The goals that you set in your outline are the tangible results that tell you that you are headed in the right direction.

Every time you accomplish one of your goals you gain more confidence and become certain that real success is just ahead. Each time that you passed another milestone all the negative beliefs that you use to have faded away. Doubt slips farther and farther away from your ears, and all you can hear now is the sound of celebration that rings down in the depth of your soul.

Think like a high achiever

I know that you are starting to feel those wheels in your head turning more and more. You have new ideas forming every day, and you are starting to get excited about the possibilities of finally being good at something. However; at the same time, a nervous feeling is lingering at the bottom of your belly because your new ideas are all over the place. You are thinking to yourself there is no possible way that I can do all these things. Yes, you can! Stop thinking like that. Stop thinking average thoughts and unmotivated rhetoric. Keep thinking like a million-aire. Yes, I said that. This book is taking your stinking thinking and turning it into successful thinking already.

You can have whatever you say, and you already learned you could have whatever you think. The secret to success is you must say what you think. In the book of Life, Jesus tells his disciples "if they have faith the size of a grain of Mustard seed they could say to this mountain be thou removed and tossed into the sea," (Matt. 17:20). What a powerful statement about saying what you believe. Let's pause here and discuss what faith truly is. I think Bishop Clarence McClendon put it best when he said, "Faith is a set of internal beliefs that demand a corresponding response."[2] In other words, you must move according to what you believe is possible. If you can dream it, you can have it because you can only dream for what you can comprehend. If you can comprehend it, then summarize it. It is your sumari zation that will give you a for success. Write your goals and begin to recite them to yourself.

The secret to success is you must say what you think

By quoting them to yourself, your goals take on a life of their own, one of power and virtue.

High Achievers follow a precise plan that is strate-gically organized. The strategic plan takes discipline to

---

[2] Bishop Clarence McClendon Preaching at Prayer Conference hosted by Bishop William Murphy Jr. Dearborn, MI. Ritz Carlton 2007.

develop. Winners understand the rules to success and strictly adhere to them. They flush every idea out to see how profitable it can be in the end. If the idea makes sense and there is a need for it, then they pursue it. Think for a moment about the wealthiest people in the world what are they known for casinos, banks, computers, movies, real estate this list goes on. The one common thing about them is they make their money in several different ways. That is why you cannot stop your dream machine to early. I know the world teaches you to focus on one thing at a time, but that is thinking average. You want to always be in a position of research and development. The more you know, the more likely you are to be successful over and over again.

A high achieving thinker does not only want to get a million from his current project, but he is always thinking about how he can make a million on his next project. I am not saying that you are not *Write your goals* successful if you do not make a *and begin to recite* million dollars I am just saying *them to yourself* why not shoot for the stars. Don't become stuck in one mode of thinking. Successful people are always thinking, and dreaming about expansion. Most people only think of earning a million as their life goal not realizing taxes will eat a lot of it up. A millionaire thinks of how to net a million and how to keep taxes low. Make sure you remember:

"An investment in knowledge always pays the best interest."

-Benjamin Franklin

One more thing I want you to keep in mind is that successful people always find a way to invest in themselves. If you are going to be successful, you must invest in yourself. Spend time going to seminars, and buying books that are going to help you progress. Develop your skills and perfect your craft to stay on the cutting edge of your industry. You want to be a valuable resource to your family and the community at large. Learn as much as you can become a student of success and earn the grades of a high achiever. Keep in mind that millionaires and high achievers are not average thinkers. Buy a notebook so that you can begin to journal your thoughts, dreams, and visions. Make sure to write in your planner a time where you have a power session with your notebook. A power session is where you sit down and brainstorm

If you are going to be successful, you must invest in yourself

and get your collective juices flowing. You will notice that every time you do this, you will get more excited about your future. Keep referencing back to your notebook every time you feel yourself getting discouraged. When you become discontent ask yourself where did you get off track. Find the distractions or recalculate a decision that caused you to veer off the road toward your goals. It does not matter if you want to be a doctor or a dancer the path to success looks the same.

Learn to speak "Success"

I was sitting in my bed thinking one day that every nationality has its own language and that every profession has its own vocabulary. Well, the same must be true about high achievers. I have found that it is not only true, but it is what signifies the arrival of a winner. Every successful person I have heard speak sounds just like the last one I heard. The topic could be different, the event could be different, but the message was the same. Certain words must be a part of your vocabulary just as there are certain words you should forget how to pronounce. You must learn how to become an effective communicator by any means necessary. Start talking like a high achiever talks and you will notice a difference in the outcomes of your conversation. Your conversations will become much more productive and informative.

High Achieving people speak with a successful tone in their voice. Have you ever noticed a successful business person who spoke with very low confidence? I surely never have. Successful people have a positive tone in their voice.

They speak with enthusiasm and energy. They make people listen to them by their demeanor and power. Communication skills are a vital tool in the life of a high achiever. Learning to not only speak the language of success but learning to use the language masterfully is a must. Successful communication will be the difference in the amount of time it takes for you to become successful in your dreams and to reach your goals.

Use whatever level of education you have and build from there. A winner's vocabulary takes much time to learn. It can be as complicated as any of Newton's Laws, Socrates' theories, or the most complex algebraic equation but you still need to learn it. This language is essential to the success of all high achievers. If you cannot speak it, you will, in fact, feel like another language is being spoken when you are in the midst of true high achievers. You will find yourself traveling down a road backward all because you did not invest in your success vocabulary bank.

You must learn how to become an effective communicator by any means necessary

Join one of your local business associations or take a class in debt management at your local recreation center for starters. Do something to move beyond average thinking and foggy insight. Anything that will help you get out of the rat race is a step in the right direction and will begin

26

to help you interpret million-dollar conversations. The point that I am trying to make is that a million dollars will not just fall from the sky and into your lap, you must reach outside your comfort zone to find it.

I know you are saying to yourself please just give me one these words or a clue to what it sounds like. Ok! The one word that I will provide you with is peace. You can achieve true peace just by being prepared. What is the definition of true peace? Peace can be defined as "'completeness,' 'wholeness,' 'well-being,' or 'welfare and peace.' It is derived from a root that means 'to be complete' or 'to be sound.'"[3] Winners seek a life of peace, as well as, success and victory. Finding peace is a fulfilling journey that reduces stress as you go. You will live a life free of pressure when you are prepared, disciplined, and focused for the assignment that you have accepted. I know this book is not your ordinary book I did not intend for it to be. I want to blend motivation, inspiration, and information in the hope of changing your thought patterns from average to successful.

Destiny Curse Words

Well, I guess I must also talk about words that are

[3] Eugene E. Carpenter and Philip W. Comfort, Holman Treasury of Key Bible Words: 200 Greek and 200 Hebrew Words Defined and Explained (Nashville, TN: Broadman & Holman Publishers, 2000), 135.

not allowed to be used in the language of high achievers as well. It is like talking to your kids; you must tell them what they can say, as well as what they are not allowed too. Every language has broken words, negative words, or curse words. In America, most parents will not allow their children to swear in public openly. We consider these four and five letter words as inappropriate. Yet we allow ourselves and our children to use words of poverty and debt continually.

There is a great vocabulary divide between those that have and those that do not. A former business coach always told our team to change the legacy of our families. We change this legacy by speaking a different language than those that went before us. We need to stop using negative four and five letter words. I hear you asking me to stop stalling and tell you these words. Ok fine. Stop using words like poor, debt, lack, less, needy, and broke to name a few. We must use words that will build our self-esteem and challenge our way of thinking.

Successful communication will be the difference in the amount of time it takes for you to become successful in your dreams and to reach your goals

The words that come out of your mouth will determine what type of doors open for you. Your level of success can be identified by the words that you use. If you speak like a high achiever, you will see that people will respond to you differently than they did when you did not. Everyone wants to be connected to people of influence and power so always speak with authority. Breaking old habits of using condescending words is difficult but necessary. Try to remove a negative word from your vocabulary a week. If you do this, you will become a more successful person in no time.

Leadership Alert:
There is no power in
empty words until action
brings them to life

③ *I'm Pregnant*

 *A*fter you have a clear road map of where you are going, you will be able to share your vision with others. Notice I did not say dream I said vision. Before we share our visions with others, we must make sure it is polished and fine-tuned. You need to refine it and revise it so that others can digest it. Please do not think this is only for people who are in business because it is not. It is for anyone who wishes to be successful in life. We all need people on our team that can help us reach our goals. No man is an island. You needed help getting here (birth), and someone will help take you away, as a matter of fact, six people will take you away; they are called pallbearers. We all need encouragement from others at different times during our journey.

The word impregnate is made up of two words that give value to its meaning. Those two words are I am pregnant. For you to impregnate others, you must be filled with something yourself first. I impregnate people all over the world with fresh ideas and energy. Therefore, I am called an urban thought architect. I am a ball of ideas and energy that burn every day at both ends of the candle. When a man impregnates a woman, he must have the

31

ability to produce life already inside of him. A man who is having a difficult time creating life will have a hard time impregnating a woman without medical help. This is true in business as well. People will be inspired by your dream when you learn how to bring life to it. You will notice that other people will begin to thank you for inspiring them to achieve their dreams.

"Our words are seeds planted into other people's lives"
– John Mason

It is imperative that we spend time understanding how our vision affects others around us. A single mother going to school will encourage her child that though they may struggle not to give up on their dreams. I remember growing up in my earlier years in a single parent home. I watched my mom get on the bus with my older sister and me. It took me some time to realize that she was taking the bus to school. I can remember my mother's first nursing graduation (notice I said first) like it was yesterday. She had the biggest smile that day as if a burden had been lifted off her shoulders. I watched my mother start climbing the corporate ladder of nursing as a single parent with a beat-up

We all need people on our team that can help us reach our goals

car who lived in the ghetto of Detroit. My mother later found happiness and got remarried only to have her new husband killed seven and a half years later. True to form my mother raised her head and her standard of living again as a single parent with a teenage boy. I watched her put me in the best of schools while she earned advanced degrees herself. My mother always encouraged me to know that life is what I make it. If I trust God and strive to do my best I could never be a failure. She impregnated me with a spirit of determination. She made sure I never settled for average. My mom made sure she challenged my thinking at an early age.

I was talking with a teenager once who believed that no one could determine what average was for him. I told him that average identifies itself by one's goals or lack thereof. I realized talking to him that the person who refuses to set goals has done so by default. By not setting goals, a person has decided that mediocrity and low achievement is acceptable for them. For those of you who were once like this, I have made it my mission that you never find yourself like this again. What you think of yourself will determine what you think of your future. I want you to say to yourself that greatness is inside of me and today I will let it out. Remember you can have what you say. This leads me to the next principle, surround yourself with talented people. The people in your tribe and inner circle must change. You cannot have the same "squad" tomorrow if it consists of people who are willing to live an average life. Do not be overprotective of your feelings either. It will take a few bad relationships to understand the value of the healthy ones. Maintain any relationship that will hold future value.

I will show you mine if you show me yours

Learn to look for certain qualities in your business and community relationships. In fact, your business relationships will carry many of the same traits as a marriage. You want to develop relationships with people who are sensitive to the needs of others. You want to find people with a positive attitude. Imagine trying to study for a final exam for college course with someone who has a negative attitude. All they will talk about is how difficult the professor is and how hard the tests usually are. Instead, study with someone who will tell you they know they are going to ace the exam. They believe that the test is going to be easy because the professor makes the class enjoyable. This is the type of person you want to be around. Find people with high self-esteem and self-worth. People who believe you should take life by the horns and ride it.

When a woman gets married, she changes her last name to the last name of her husband. On the other hand, when a successful woman gets married she often put a hyphen behind her maiden name so that her identity does not get lost. You must marry success and add success to your name. I have already told you that you can have what you dream when you speak it and believe it. Whenever you speak your dream speak your new married name. Instead of saying I am a student, say I am a successful student. Instead of I am an entrepreneur say I am a successful entrepreneur. Instead of I work in sales say I am a successful salesperson. It is surprising how this will begin to cause positive energy to not only flow through your mind but your body, as well giving you a sense of achievement.

When a woman gets married, she is excited about her new transition. She is ready to face the challenges of merging two lives in a new home and developing a complex yet trusting set of values with her husband. This marriage will be one of the hardest tasks she will face in life, but she meets it with excitement and joy. The bride does not leave the church thinking it is going to get harder from here. She leaves that church enjoying the moment with no thought about what is to come in the future years. You know why this is so easy for the bride and very difficult for the rest of us? Before the bride became a bride, she was woman who had committed to a relationship with someone else. She had already wondered in her mind what would it be like to marry this guy. She had thoughts about how many children they would have and where they would live. Therefore, when her boyfriend decides it is time to propose, she is not surprised because she had planned for this day from the beginning. As she walks down the isle of celebration after saying her wedding vows, she already knows in her heart how the story will unfold. She knows she will have a successful marriage.

As you begin to surround yourself with successful people you will start to see many familiar qualities. High Achievers have an inner drive that seems to be pushing them. They maintain a healthy self-image and a positive attitude. These complex people always bring something of value into any relationship. There is something important to remember. When you are trying to build a healthy relationship with individuals that are truly successful, you must lose your grade school mentality. You remember that girl or boy from grade school that you told I will show you mine if you show me yours. Well, that type of thinking will not work now. You must upgrade your thought process. Learning to become better at a task requires first admitting that you are not good at it. Do not be afraid to ask for help or support. Become vulnerable to those who are going to pour into your life and strengthen you. Stop being paranoid about people stealing from you.

High achievers only associate with other high achievers. You must make a great first impression and show that you are a person of success and value from the very beginning. If you are waiting to see if the other person is a high achiever or not before you put your value on display, you will only find out when you are watching them from behind, traveling down the road of success.

Let's get right to it

You need to have a let's get right to it attitude. There are several different types of relationships that you will find yourself. Some of these relationships will last longer than others. I once heard a preacher say, "relationships are like a glass of milk. They are healthy for you when used in the proper season, but can become deadly for you when used after the expiration date". You must understand that not every relationship will last a lifetime. Some relationships will be just for a project while others will be for a much more extended period. With this thought in mind, you must maximize every aspect of the relationship from the very beginning. We have all met people who from the day we met them we knew there was something special about them. You want to make sure that you are one of those people. Develop into a person of inspiration and positive impact. Become an expert in whatever you do so that others can sense the value that is deep down inside of you. Remember that everyone wants to be connected to an expert. It makes them feel successful and well connected.

Positive friends will help you to live a supercharged life. One day I was driving my car, and I went into the store for about an hour. Upon returning to my car, it would not start up. It was a warm summer day, and I was not really in the mood to be stuck at the mall. While I waited for roadside assistance to come and give my battery a boost, I checked all my doors to make sure that my children did not leave one open by mistake. They were all closed properly. However, I did notice that my dome light which normally would shine brightly was very dim even with all the doors shut. It then dawned on me that I must have turned the light on by accident. Well needless to say I opened the car back up and turned the light off. I decided instead of waiting outside for roadside assistance I would go back into the mall and enjoy the atmosphere.

See I knew that sitting in a hot car during the summer would ruin my day. I would rather be in the middle of the action instead of outside in the parking lot. That day in the mall I met some fascinating people that I could tell right away were high achievers. After about an hour of walking and talking I went back out to my car, and it started right up. There are two things I learned that day. The first thing was to always put myself in a place where I can maximize the circumstances. The second was that all our batteries get a little low sometimes, but we must be able to recharge ourselves when there is no one around to do it for us.

Give me your best

I will admit that I am a demanding person. In fact, many would say that I am very demanding. I believe that is one of the qualities that make me a successful speaker and an excellent trainer. I only want to be around people who are going to give their very best effort in everything that they do. I hate to lose. Losing puts a sour taste in my mouth. I am a very competitive person. I got A's in school because I did not want somebody else to be better than me. People know that when they work on my team, 100% is not enough. I want you to give a 110% toward every task. I was once asked if this caused some people to avoid working with me. My response was I hope so. I developed a red carpet mentality. Only people who are willing to strive for a particular standard or quality will desire to work on my team. If I am honest, those are the people I most desire to with alongside.

You see as a high achiever I do not have time to wait on people who have to be motivated to give their best or to use their talents. I want people around me who are already prepared to do that. If you give me the best that you got, I will do the same for you every time. I know that most of you have heard that a referral is the highest compliment that you can give a salesperson. The only way a salesperson is going to get a referral is by providing their customers the very best service they can. Many people sell the same products, in fact, I learned that most products sell themselves. A salesperson must go above and beyond what is considered normal by their customer if they want to receive referrals.

While working as a real estate agent one year I learned this principle first hand. It seemed as if every time I went to the office that my phone did not ring with new business. I always had to make calls and leave messages if I wanted my phone to ring. One day I decided to begin networking and showing every potential customer I met why I was the best agent in town. Those customers began calling and next thing I knew I was listing one house after another. The more interesting thing was that each customer was so pleased with my attitude that they referred me to their family and friends before I even sold their house. Things began going so good that I had to turn my cell phone off when I got home if I wanted to enjoy my evenings. I later got more business by being in the mall, a restaurant, gym, etc. than I did sitting at my desk. When you give people your best, they will, in turn, reward you for your efforts.

You must become demanding as well. I am not telling you to act obnoxious and unbearable. Just become a fiery ball of positive energy who always expects to get excellent results. Never settle for less than what you originally intended to have. You should always have high expectations for yourself and those around you. People must know that you are serious about your dreams and vision. You should look for the qualities of a high achiever in a person if you are going to let them into your inner circle of influence. Everyone is not able to be a part of your inner circle of success. This would be considered your board of directors of your life. You should have person for each of the foundational components of human existence in your life. You need a person that will function as a spiritual guide, a business coach that helps you reach professional goals, and a personal trainer that enables you to maintain proper physical balance. These people must be successful in their respective areas, as well as be people of purpose and destiny.

I am glad I met you

I am glad I met you is a phrase that should become very familiar to you. It is a phrase that you should utter to others. High achievers will always have an immediate impact on your life. They will both inspire and encourage you to raise your attitude and expectation of your efforts. These are the people that will leave you in awe when you watch them. They will cause self-doubt to creep in momentarily and then you will begin to feel empowerment burst through the essence of your existence. They challenge you to believe in the impossible and to reach for the stars. People of high success make you believe that if you follow the plan, you will become invincible to the challenges of the unseen world. They fill your notebook with much-needed information and your brain with knowledge. The day that you meet them or sit in one of their seminars becomes one of the greatest days in your life.

The second time you should hear this phrase is when you positively impact others. This is what other people should say to you. You must learn to become a positive influence on the lives of others. The keyword you must learn at this stage is "pour out." You should pour out everything that you learn. Do not become a reservoir that holds onto everything that others have poured into you, but be like a river that will pour out into another body of water. You are already on the road to greatness. You know what it takes to be a high achiever now. Make sure other people get the same opportunity that you did. Share your success with those who need to hear it. Remember that it should become your desire to help other people think like you.

I'm pregnant again

The word impregnate has become one of my favorite words. It is defined in the dictionary as "to infuse the principle of conception; to make pregnant, to communicate the virtues or one thing to another, as in pharmacy, by mixture, digestion."[1] You should get excited by the definition of this word. When you are around highly successful people, they impart into you the very qualities they posse. Think of it like this you started out with a dream but did not know how to put all the pieces together. After having a conversation with a high achiever, you will now know how to frame your outline. They will help you through the two steps we call "write it" and "summarize it."

A high achiever will help you learn where to place your focus and how to lean on your strengths. Before

---

[1] Webster, 1828

43

you know it, you will be pregnant with your idea all over again. They will cause you to enlarge your dream and your vision. You will raise your level of expectation once again. You will sound like the little engine that could because you will find yourself saying I think I can, I think I can. Whenever you begin to feel down and out and as if your dream is not possible, call up a mentor or coach and take them to lunch. They will provide you with an instant shot of energy. That will help you begin to think like a winner.

Impregnate is an action word. When you impregnate someone, you have filled them with a substance they need to reproduce life. Look at the power in that statement. This book should impregnate you with power to produce your dreams, walk in your vision and become a high achiever. This is possible because I am imparting to you the very things that have been deposited in me. When a deposit has been successful, it creates life inside the receiver. Success is not a magical formula; it is a well-defined life-style. A planned pregnancy is an exciting experience for the expecting family. Notice that a planned pregnancy is expected, so should it be with the positive outcomes of your life. Expect success!

Everyone needs a person to nudge them now and then. I attended a seminar with a great motivational speaker Jonathan Edison. His seminar learning to speak savvy is one that I would highly recommend for anyone who wants to improve their ability to communicate. In this class, we discussed me writing a book. I knew I was supposed to write a book over twelve years ago. I am a high energy person, and I am always on the go. I never had time to sit down and write a book. I mention to him how I had just gathered some of my signature messages together on a couple CD's and sent it to a transcriber. I knew this was my easiest way of getting my message into a book. However, Jonathan encouraged me just to sit down and write it. I had been told that before, but he put it in such a way that it inspired me to do it. Two days later my children were on a break from school. This meant that my usual routine would be interrupted. Instead of looking at their vacation as an obstacle in my schedule I used it to start writing this book. He pushed me to do something big that I was making excuses for not doing.

I have given presentations all over the world for years so the information was inside of me. I sat down and thought about what I wanted to write. I summarized it so I could decide who it would be useful for and then I outlined it. As I began writing this book, I believed more and more that it was possible for me to finish. My children started to

Success is not a magical formula; it is a well-defined lifestyle

45

look over my shoulders and read as I typed all day and all night. They were more excited about the book than I was. My wife jumped on the bandwagon and began to encourage me and tell me how excited she was watching me do it. When you are impregnated with something you are excited, and energy becomes contagious.

A good friend of my mine, songwriter, and singer James "Corey" Robinson, asked me to take a trip with him while I was working on this book. I was not going to do it at first, but something down inside of me told me to go ahead and go. During our drive Corey let me hear the unedited version of his newest project. It is very inspirational. We began discussing what he was trying to accomplish with his CD. I started sharing with him about this new book that I was writing and the reason why I finally began putting it together. He was encouraged by this book and told me to hurry up and finish so that he could buy a copy. We then discussed me appearing on one of the songs on his project. It is important to be around people who are pregnant with promise because they will encourage you to continue with the assignment you have begun. I also learned when we take too long finishing projects those who love us may never see it. We lost Corey before I completed writing this book. He was never able to finish his project either. We let life and other people's dreams supersede ours.

I do not mean to seem as if I am bragging about myself, but after being encouraged by Jonathan and Corey, I came home and called a business partner who owned media company. We discussed a few new concepts that his business was just starting to put in place. His excitement was so contagious that I began to get excited with him. He helped put together a third website for my umbrella of companies as well as add new concepts to my business that will allow me to be on the cutting edge as a pastor and Professional Speaker. He was equipping me with tools that the major players in my industry would dream of having.

See how his success began to cause me to expand my dream even further. I have not deviated from my plan I have just made it even broader so that I can maximize my earning potential. That is a phrase that I love to hear. Why don't you read this phrase out loud "Earning Potential?" When you are impregnated by others that are successful, you become pregnant with possibilities once again. You should always be giving birth to one idea while you are still discovering new ideas. You can be great if you just learn to "Think Like It."

Leadership Alert:
"You will be as small as your controlling desire, as great as your dominate aspiration."
-James Allen

④ *Stay* <u>*Focused*</u>

I did what you said, now what?

*Y*ou have probably noticed the style of this book ever so slightly changing as you read. I have done this on purpose. I believe that as you read a little bit each day and listen to one of the tapes or CD's that I have available that your confidence should be increasing. At this point, you should be trying different principles that I have outlined in this book. Please do not try to read this book in one week because if you do, you will become disappointed with your results. Read a little each day and then apply the principle that you have learned. Growth happens as you take one step at a time. Read a little and then implement one principle as you develop new habits.

I did not write this book with the intent of you becoming an overnight success. Please keep in mind that success does not happen overnight. It takes many days and hours of hard work to become successful. I can relate this most to my life as a real estate agent. In real estate, you work today to find a client next week or maybe next month. You then work with that client for days or weeks perhaps even months before they decide on a home. After their decision, you will still have to wait for ten or maybe forty-five days or so for the deal to close and for your paycheck to be cut. If you ever stop working hard, your success will come to an end, and you will have to start all over.

Hard work and practice are essential factors to the level of success you will achieve. Everyone must practice. I practice as a professional speaker every day. My mother used to tell me "practice makes perfect." I teach my children that when you practice, you do not have to be nervous. Repetition and confidence are coupled together for those who perform at peak levels.

I remember when my daughter was training to be a professional dancer. She knew at eleven that she really wanted to dance. She was already traveling across the country dancing on a team or with the dance school she attended. There was a recital where she did well, but I could tell she did not perform at peak level. I asked her later was she nervous and she said to me "just a little" that's my daughter's way of saying yes. I asked her why was she nervous and she said to me, "I was not comfortable with my routine because I had not practiced it enough." Two weeks later she performed with a team at a concert and she shined as she usually does. She practiced this particular routine several times before the event. If my then eleven-year-old daughter understood that preparation calms nerves and release stress anyone can learn that very same thing.

One day I was on a phone interview with the president of an up and coming speaker bureau. During the interview, I was asked about overcoming nervousness. The president said to me that all speakers get nervous and the bigger the crowd, the more nervous they become. I disagreed and told him that when you are the best at your craft, there is no need to be nervous. Preparation calms nervousness and relieves stress. Standing on stage in front of a small audience is no less intimidating than standing on a large stage. The size of the stage does not make a difference the level of preparation does. When you practice the same thing every day as if you are on stage you will not be nervous when it is time to perform. I declined the offer to join that bureau. My desire is to partner with other creatives who think like me.

The gift of opportunity

A person who is not nervous is a person who feels free in their spirit and emotions. Nervousness will have you feeling as if you are trapped inside of a prison. I have seen great speakers stand before crowds sweating with fear and intimidation. I always think to myself that person is not prepared to do their best today. When I am before a crowd and fully prepared, I feel calm as if I was out on the lake fishing. The only time I am even the slightest bit nervous is when I have not prepared for the task at hand. I like to relax the night before I have a presentation or big deal. I can only do that if I have prepared myself all the previous days leading up to an event. If I have to take a big test, I go out and celebrate the day before the test. Why? Well because I know that I have already prepared to succeed so nothing on the test will be a surprise to me. Success is a mindset, and my mind is already set on succeeding.

One year I decided to follow up on one of my goals. I always wanted to obtain my insurance producers license, but I always put it off. One year I decided to give myself a deadline for getting my license before the year was over. Unfortunately, December came, and I had not yet reached my goal. Two good friends of mine came and presented an opportunity for me to join a financial services organization. I joined mostly because I wanted to obtain my producers license. Of course, my schedule became an issue, but I forced myself to work around it. I decide to take the one-week course they offered the week before Christmas. The class was Tuesday through Thursday. While I was in the class, the teacher told us to call and schedule our state examine. Well, most of my classmates listen and scheduled their test for two weeks away. In fact, this is what the school recommends. However, on that Wednesday of class, I called and scheduled my exam for that upcoming Friday. I did not tell anyone in the class because I did not want them to discourage me. When Friday came, I was pumped up, and yes, I passed the state exam. I was able to do this because I was focused and determined to reach my goal. My holiday week was exciting and rewarding not because of gifts that I received from others but because of the gift I gave myself. I gave myself the gift of opportunity.

Stay Focused

It takes focus to practice or study the same thing repeatedly. You think you are prepared for the test but study some more. You think you have memorized the script but rehearse it again. Focus on the task at hand. Your current assignment is preparation. When it is time for me to speak, I must be ready. I cannot come up with thoughts as I go. I must follow my plan and stick to what has been proven to be successful. You must have a plan. We worked on your plan when we developed your outline and your goals. Your outline defines your objective; it tells you what you are trying to accomplish. Your goals are your landmarks on the road to success. Every time you reach one of your goals you know you are headed in the right direction. Once you notice that you are not consistently achieving your goals, begin to evaluate where you have fallen short and make adjustments. You have fallen asleep at the wheel on the highway to success. The goals have not changed, but your focus has. If you are reaching some of your goals and not others, hold yourself accountable for your temporary setbacks.

Staying focused is a challenging thing to do. Many people struggle while reading not because they cannot comprehend but because they do not stay focused. Focusing is a habit that successful people must develop. It must become second nature. A person who is not focused will never accomplish the goals that have real value or meaning. There will always be distractions that arise and obstacles that get in the way. However, these trials can be overcome with hard work, determination, and focus. Remain focused on the task at hand and keep a positive attitude. Staying focus will reward you with long-term success.

The world that we live in today emphasizes express services. You can even use your credit or debit card at fast food restaurants today. This has caused us to become overly infatuated with material things opposed to real success. For example, many people talk on their cell phones while driving. Even though we all know which streets to turn on when we go to work in the morning, we will often miss our turn if we are talking on our cell phones. Just a simple thing as talking on the phone can cause you to be delayed five maybe ten minutes while you turn around and come back to a place you always go. By talking on the phone, you have taken your eyes off the landmarks that you usually would identify as significant on your route to your destination. This is what our goals do for us. They tell us that we are on the path to success. Your goals tell you to make a turn at the next intersection, or you have five more miles to go. If you miss your landmarks you will not be left wondering how much far you have to go?

Don't give up on your dream

The most common reason for people not being successful is because they give up. It does not matter if you are nine or ninety-nine years old there is still a purpose for your life. Do not let anyone discourage you including yourself. Every time you feel depressed remember the story of the postage stamp. A postage stamp is ripped from its home licked and stuck on a letter. This postage stamp knows that once it is called into duty, it shall never return to a place that is familiar again. The letter that carries the postage stamp knows the destination, but the stamp has no idea of where it is going. However, the postage stamp knows it is qualified to carry out the task because of the value its creator gave him. With that in mind, the postage stamp sticks to the letter through all kind of adversity until it reaches a place called "there." You need to have the tenacity of the postage stamp. Stop looking for things to come easy, face adversity head-on. If you can dream it, you can have it. You believed in your dream enough to reach for it, now keep on believing until you arrive at success.

Success is born at night while you are sleep. Your dreams give you the ability to see into your innermost thoughts and ideas. It is in your dreams where creativity and genius can be discovered. I am amazed at the amount of confidence people express in their dreams. Even people with low self-esteem have a sense of heroism in their dreams. I believe this is because everyone has that feeling of being able to control the out come of the events he or she dream. Control is a power ful tool for high achievers and dreamers. Control makes a person feel as though fear can not prevail over them.

You must learn how to become an effective communicator by any means necessary

I was in a meeting one day where a woman was determined to make us all believe that she was not successful because she did not have any money. She thought that

56

it takes money to make money. She begins to explain that she needed money to create her niche and to market her brand. She went on to say not only did she need money but anyone who wanted to be successful needed money as well. "Rags to riches stories always leave out a valuable piece of the story," she exclaimed almost in tears. After listening to her, I came up with one conclusion. It is not that she needed money to be successful she needed a dream to fuel her passion. This woman lacked money, but she was not desperate enough yet. She wanted sympathy from me not help to reach her goals. Until she wanted to win as much as she wanted to breathe, she would continue to make excuses for her lack of success. Eric Thomas says, "When you want to succeed as bad as you want to breathe, then you will be successful."[1]

Money is not the only resource that dreamers need to become successful. In fact, money is not at the top of the list of needs to run a productive business. You must become a resource manager first. Take an inventory of all your dreams and ideas and then leverage your gifts and talents to bring you the vital support that you really need. When you have high desire to succeed coupled with a dream that you are passionate about, you will not be denied success. You will know that you can control the outcome and there is not anything or anyone who can

[1] Stephen Gardner, Eric Thomas Wisdom: 169 Rules on How to Succeed as Bad as You Want to Breathe (2016), 2-3.

stop you but you.

Most people are like the lady I just mention stuck in a mode of thought that will not cause dreams to become a reality. We all want to believe in the impossible but have difficulty seeing beyond the obstacle of finances that stand in our way. However, the one thing any successful dreamer must have is leverage. You must learn how to leverage the things that you do well so that they benefit you and your business ideas. Your dreams will only go as far as you take them. You must remember that you are in control of your dreams and that your dreams do not control you. Your dreams give you the ability to see the finished product. They allow you to start with the end in mind. That lady could not understand how leveraging her skills would eliminate her need for finances. She is still trying to figure out where she will get the money from to begin her business while others who were in the same room have already started down the road to success. I tried to help her realize that she is her business. She is focused on a product that has yet to be manufactured instead of focusing on her ability to sell herself.

I thank God that I started out as a real estate investor at a young age. Real estate helped me learn that I did not need my own money to make money. I began my career by leveraging and bartering everything that I could. I later learned that was the "American Way" of doing business. I still use the leveraging principle in my business and real estate deals today. As I began to move forward in my real estate sales career, I did not have much money at first. I had to find a way to get customers and close sales. Gary Keller had just written the book, "The Millionaire Real Estate Agent" where he discusses the value of leveraging for business. At this point leveraging really began to work for me. I learned how to maximize the potential of a network, a dream, and passion for producing income for me and my family.

The rat race will overtake you if you let it. Many people die from the stress and frustration associated with the race. A true dreamer will find a way out of the rat race. A successful dreamer will become resourceful in their attempt to achieve financial freedom. Don't give up on your dream because of your inability to see beyond your current economic situation. It does not always take your money to bring your dreams to life. It is important to remember that if you can dream it, you can have it.

Everyone has a breaking point, but no one should ever experience it. We should never live our lives with unnecessary pressure. Accountability has its place, but never let accountability become abuse either from you or others. Relationships are supposed to be healthy and prosperous. Make sure you do not give up on your dreams because of the unnecessary pressure of others.

Reach your goals at your own pace. For indeed you are the one that must live with the choice that you are making. Focus, is a person of greatness most used quality. Focus allows you to stay positive and energetic. By remaining focused, you are telling all onlookers to take notice and recognize that you are determined to reach your goals come hell or high water.

For most of us when we think of our dreams we do not feel that we can have them now. We think that we must wait for some future date to obtain our dreams. We act as if the future is a date that we can find on the calendar. The future is not a date or time; it is a moment of opportunity. The future is now. The future will come rather you want it to or not. Every day when you wake up, you are in your future. Every passing second is a part of your future. You must learn how to see your future now.

⑤ *Power Principles*

 *T*here is an incredible untapped energy inside of you called power. This power can make you a dynamic force in the world. All your dreams, goals and aspirations must be fueled by this power. Continue to feed this energy source within you so that it can carry you to destinations that you have not even dreamed were possible yet. What is this energy you ask? It is called life.

We all have been given life and the ability to reproduce it. You have the power of life in you, and you must begin to give life to things around you. Give life to your dreams and vision. Life is so powerful that you cannot lock it in a box. The power of life cannot be measured by any measuring stick. Measuring the life of another is impossible. You can only measure yours by the things you give life.

There are four power principles that I like to use on a regular basis. All my coaching sessions are built around these four principles the four power principles are:

1. Think Like What I Want

2. Have Contagious Faith

3. Impregnate Others

4. Read to Grow

I believe these are pillars to building success. In fact, I do not see how you can be successful without utilizing these principles. Each one carries its very own unique characteristics. High achievers understand the value of these principles and follow them on a regular basis. I also use these with the five "its" of success I believe with both sets of principles combined I have set myself up for an enjoyable journey down the road of success.

Think It

Our thoughts are continually shaping us. We must block out all negative thoughts because they carry the potential to sabotage your dreams and goals. Remember this, "But the things that come out of a person's mouth come from the heart, and these defile them," (Matt.15:18). Words are what shape our destiny. Our thoughts help us calculate the risk of our actions, "as a man thinketh in his heart so is he," (Pr. 23:7). Your thoughts have a power all of their own. Unlock that power and let it flow. You are not able to achieve anything unless you give birth to the thought first. You must think it, to even attempt it. Your thoughts can change the direction of your life overnight. Many people find themselves working on jobs they do not like because as they would say their "heart is not in it." Their working in one place today while they wish and dream to do something different with their lives. When you were a child, your teachers tried to make you think by asking you a simple question. What do you want to be when you grow up? Have you asked yourself that question lately? What do you want to be or do? The reason why you have not achieved your dream is that you stop thinking about it. Do yourself a favor and start thinking again about things that matter to your future.

See It

Seeing your dreams and thoughts ahead of time is essential. When you see your dreams, you frame them. The best part about seeing your dream is that you can change the parts that you do not like. Seeing your dream also makes it more believable. You believe the things you see much easier than the things you do not. Your mind is visual and will create little pictures or frames of your thoughts that will last a lifetime if you let them. Whenever you get discouraged just remember the things that you saw in your mind. You have heard the saying that a picture is worth a thousand words so what are your pictures saying to you? See yourself going to the next level and then go after it. Create a vision board or a dream board as

I like to call it. Put everything you want to accomplish in one section and then place pictures of the obstacles you will overcome beneath them. Look at this board daily to remind yourself why you are working so hard.

Speak It

Your mountains know your voice. Whenever you face trouble speak it out of your way. If you would say to this mountain move, it must listen.[1] Every organized religion would teach you this in some form or another. What they do not teach you is how to walk in your destiny despite the odds. The easiest way to replace negative thoughts is to speak positive ones. You can control your thought pattern by speaking positive affirmations to yourself on a regular basis. Words are like little containers that carry your thoughts and commands to various destinations much like a boomerang. They always have a way of coming back to you. Whatever you sow into your environment will come back to you. Speak words of life and power, and they will return the virtues thereof.

Years ago, I wrote a booklet on real estate. It was horribly produced but packed full of powerful nuggets. The book was reviewed in publications I had never heard of before. I received excellent reviews and words of en-

[1] My interpretation of Matthew 11:23

couragement. I was called things such as guru, genius, and ahead of my time which was inspiring. I printed these words out and put them in a place where I could read them often to remind me of the people lives that I had touched. I also received a tremendous amount of criticism. Reading the positive words about me encouraged me to speak positive things over my dreams. I use my voice to drown out the noise from the critics. Critics who are often sitting on the sidelines as you are passing them by can only affect you if you take time to stop and listen.

Walk It

There is a song I heard while in the store one day that said, now walk it out. We must learn how to walk out our thoughts and dreams. Many would call this walking in your destiny. I do not care what you call it just make sure you are walking in it. Trust yourself enough to know that when you walk in the things you believe in you will see amazing results. This principle takes a lot of faith and determination to accomplish.

People of greatness do not wait until becoming successful to look like it. They appear successful long before success ever arrives in their lives. When they do become successful, you will only see subtle changes in their behavior because they have prepared for it the entire time. Success is something that they emulate so they understand the poise and posture they must have. Stick your chest out and put your head back and walk with confidence. Know that your life is changing for the best. Do not allow setbacks and obstacles to cause you to become depressed and non-responsive. Walk through your life knowing that you are attracting greatness, because you have started down the roadway of success.

Believe it.

I believe in the impossible. My dreams are so big that I never give them a chance to get old. Whenever it seems as if I am getting close to achieving my dreams I force myself to expand them further. I give myself a reason to stretch my faith and to test my resolve. I like having a challenge or a goal to reach. My goals are what push me to greatness. Success does not come because you sit by the window looking for it. You will only have success by driving to where success is and picking it up. I know I can have whatever I believe in so I think as big as I possibly can.

A lady once told me, "seeing is believing." I said to

her you are absolutely correct. She thought that because of whom I am that I would disagree with her. In fact, she had expected me to give her a lecture regarding faith.

Instead, she was floored by what I shared with her. I told her that was a principle by which I lived my life. The principle is also the basis of most of my presentations. However, we do have one philosophical difference. I believe that's why we must dream big dreams because once I see it I know I can have it. I do not believe we must see it with our eyes in the natural. We must be able to see it in our dreams. We can have whatever we comprehend and envision. This lady was amazed that I was not going to jump down her throat about her thoughts. I told her I did not come to condemn her thoughts but to expand them.

The five "its" of success are dream it, write it, summarize it, outline it, and believe it. If you learn how to apply these principles success will find its way to you. High achievers such as you find ways to apply these rules to every endeavor in their lives. I want you to remember to learn balance. Do not become a public success and a private failure. It will mean absolutely nothing if you become successful in business but fail at being a parent or spouse. Begin to use these rules and principles today and watch things in your life begin to change.

Attitude, Aptitude, Altitude

I hope by now you understand your attitude means everything. You will only go as far as your attitude. A positive attitude will help shape your integrity. Your attitude speaks volumes about your character. It amazes me how many people work in customer service yet have a poor attitude. Learn to smile even when you do not feel like it. You must also learn how to talk with a smile. People can tell a lot about you from your voice. Make people feel as if you appreciate them even though they may be aggravating you. The law of customer service teaches us that the customer is always right. Everyone you meet is a customer. Some of you are saying to yourself that is not true because I am not in sales. Listen to me we are all in sales.

We all want someone to invest in us or something we believe. Your daughter has girls scout cookies to sell. Your son's track team has candy to sell. Your church has skating tickets for sale. You decide to interview for a new job. The task does not matter the approach is the same. Your attitude will open doors for you when you make people feel like you are happy to be knocking at the door of opportunity. Try it today. Make sure you smile at everyone you see today if when it

A positive attitude will help shape your integrity

feels odd and unnecessary.

Aptitude is defined in the dictionary as, "a natural or acquired disposition for a particular purpose, or tendency to a particular action or effect; readiness in learning; docility."[2] Whenever I think about aptitude, I always think about what my real estate coach taught me. My late real estate mentor told me, "that no one cares how much you know until he or she knows how much you care." I found this to be a profound statement of life. People are always leery of positive people. The reason why you wonder? Well, because positive people are rare these days. An informed, positive person always seems to be selling something or standing up for some cause. This person is not the norm in our everyday society. I want you to become that person. Education and research are the pillars on which you will start your journey. You must always be on the cutting edge of your expertise. Let people know that you have the information and that you are willing to share it.

Yes, there will be some that won't like you, but you are not looking to keep company with them. When you start down the path of high achievement you won't have to call your friends and inform them. All your friends not headed where you are going will find the next exit off

[2] Noah Webster, A Dictionary of the English Language (London, Black, Young, and Young, 1833)

the road. That is ok; do not feel upset over it. You cannot waste your time focusing on unproductive people. Think about it this way, you are a tree, and you judge a tree by the fruit it bears. If the people around you do not bear fruit, then they are not fruitful for you. I am not telling you to end a friendship with anyone. I am merely saying if your friends choose not to grow you should not allow them to invest a lot into your thoughts. If you do, it will not be long before old thought patterns along with that old lifestyle sneak its ugly head up in your life again. You can learn and accomplish great things; do not let people take it from you.

My mom still tells me to this day that the sky is the limit. She continues to remind me that I can be anything that I want to be. If I tell my mother I want to live on the planet Mars her response would be I am sure you will find a way to do it. I never knew the power of altitude. When you work to be the best at your craft you never believe anyone is above you. I do not know what a corporate glass ceiling looks like honestly. I heard the definition of it but refuse to believe it can contain me. I believe that people live under a personal ceiling. I know that discrimination and politics exist everywhere. However, I also know that self-confidence overcomes all strongholds and barriers. You must believe that you are gifted, talented, and informed. Those three things together are a deadly combination to anyone who opposes your dreams and visions.

You must come to a place where your presence alone demands a response from other people. It is funny to me when people call me on the phone such as telemarketers and say you speak with such authority. They then ask me what I do for a living. It stops them in their tracks they called to sell me something, but they end up learning something in return. I speak with authority because I believe that everybody has something in them that I need and all I have to do is bring it out of them. I have confidence in myself that's why I speak with such a firm tone. I am not rude or crass with people. I speak in a friendly way, and they can hear my smile over the phone. Reach for the sky, and shot for the stars you just may find yourself on the moon. No one can tell *When you work* you how high you can go or what *to be the best* you cannot achieve. Keep pressing *at your craft* forward toward success, and I will *you never believe* see you at the top. *anyone is above you*

Leadership Alert:
"Do one thing every day
that scares you."
-Mary Schmich

⑥ *Friend Or Foe?*

Who Shapes Your Thinking?

*T*he biggest problem with our society is the lack of fathers. Fathers were designed to be instructive. Their whole purpose is to help give us identity and self-worth. A man does not know who he is entirely without knowing the origins of his parents. It is this way in all aspects of life. In the life of those who reach greatness and in the business world we give parents a different name. We call them mentors or coaches.

The job description is basically the same and it is not gender specific. A mentor is supposed to help you develop and understand how you can become successful at any given task. Mentors teach us how to walk in our field of expertise and how to speak the vocabulary. For example, if you want to learn how to think like an investor you will learn it best from a mentor. Someone that will help you perfect your expertise and increase your trajectory.

We all need mentors. A mentor will give you a definite pattern of success. They do not even have to be an expert in what you do. In my opinion working with an actual mentor has equal value four years of college courses. Most people would jump at the chance to be mentored by Warren Buffett. Why? Because Warren Buffett is a proven winner that seems to succeed at everything he touches. Remember that high achievers are disciplined and focused. They work hard, and they practice. High achievers prepare for the when and not the what.

"Experience tells you what to do; confidence allows you to do it." — Stan Smith, Tennis Champion

Prepare For The When, Not The What

I remember the first time I spoke on this subject, the people in the audience looked at me very strange when I said prepare for the when and not the what. They could not understand what I meant in the beginning, but as I laid the foundation, it began to become more evident for them. Most of us have been taught to save our money so that we can buy a car or a house. The funny thing is that when you finally get the money, there never seems to be any good deals available. I believe this is because you are prepared for the "what" you desire to accomplish. I believe you should prepare for the "when" this is the time that the thing you desire is most available. You should become an expert on the stuff you want. When you can provide valid information about a subject as well as show your competence in the specific area you will flourish. Successful people will now seriously consider investing in you.

The thing that high achievers understand is that money works for them even when the money they use is not their own. This is why business moguls such as Jeff Bezos, Russell Simmons, and Bill Gates to name a few always find a way to manufacture more money. Money seems to be attracted to them, and they never seem to be without it. They all learned to give as well as earn money. You want a mentor who understands these principles.

When you have prepared for the when and not the what, you set your mind to search for opportunities. There are those who seem to just walk in favor and opportunity. Preparation is the first step to attracting favor. I am not looking to buy a house or car but having money saved in the bank will allow me to do so if a deal too good to refuse is available. Maybe you think that will never work for you, but it will and it can. If you were looking for a publishing deal with a big publisher when would you write the book? Are you going to wait for them to knock on your door and they never heard your name? That is a farfetched idea, right? If you had your book written and ready you could submit your proposal if you heard the publisher was seeking a specific genre. Preparing the manuscript ahead of time, positions you for the long-term success you desire and deserve. A finished product will generally sell better than an idea.

Confidence says I am preparing today for an opportunity that I know will become available soon. When do you become an author? You become an author after you commit to being one. In his blog, Jeff Goins writes about this concept when he interviewed Steven Pressfield. When presented the question when do you become a writer Steven reply was, "You are a writer when you tell yourself you are. No one else's opinion matters. Screw them. You are when you say you are."[1] Those words are the epitome of self-confidence and preparing for your future.

It takes research and knowledge to prepare adequately. You must learn when and how to kick open the door of opportunity. The right mentor will help you learn when the opportunity is right for you to advance down the path toward success. You should also keep in mind the law of attraction. As you do your research and prepare, you will begin to attract the very thing you are chasing. Preparation will place you in front of open doors before you are ready to walk through them. Pick the right mentor and watch your finances begin to grow as business opportunities become available.

[1] Jeff Goins, The Only Real Way to Become an Author (Goins Writer Blog) www.goinswriter.com/become-a-writer accessed 01/21/17

Friend or Foe

There are times when you will wonder if your mentor is a friend or a foe. When they try to teach you principles like the last one I shared you will wonder if they are a friend or not. These principles challenge the very way we are familiar with thinking. Old thought patterns must go away. You must change the way you view things from this point forward. A mentor is a friend from the aspect that you can call on them in a time of need. They will give you sound advice and encouragement when needed. Your mentor should also push you outside your comfort zone. The mentor you chose should remind you of a parent in that they tell you the truth even when you do not want to hear it. It is important that your mentor be honest with you.

Good criticism is always needful from a person who cares about your success. One day after I was done speaking I had a person tell me, "Carter you are too arrogant when you deliver your messages," that statement bothered me. I did not want people to think I was arrogant. I was very hurt when I heard this comment. I began listening to my tapes and CD's so that I could hear what may have some sense of arrogance in it. Then I spoke with one of my mentors, and he told me not to receive criticism from every who provides it. The lesson that I learned here was that you must consider who the criticizer is. In this case, the person criticizing me wishes they could be doing what I am doing, and the person mentoring me was already doing it and more. My mentor helped me realize that confidence is not arrogance unless you make others feel as if they cannot obtain what you have.

Mentors are demanding by nature, and you should expect poking and prodding from them. The mentor you select should have substantial experience or success in their field. Never let anyone mentor you who have not at least started down the road way of success. Successful people as we discussed in a previous chapter expect you to give your very best every time. You should never say this is the best that I can do. That is not true. You can always do better than you have before. There is always something else that you can perfect. Learn or research something new to add value to yourself and your purpose. A mentor that cares about your success or failure will never let you settle for being ordinary. If your mentor is always your friend, then ask yourself if you need to find another mentor.

Keep in mind that your mentor is building their dream as well. Make sure you do not choose a mentor who is still celebrating past success without any plan of expansion. High achievers attract other high achievers so make a list of the type of people you want in your circle of influence. You must then ask the question, are these people in my mentor's sphere of influence and if not why? If your Mentor is a mover and a shaker, then their associates will be as well. Select a mentor who has a mentor because this will ensure your personal growth as well. Do not allow a person to pour into your life who does not have someone pouring into his or her.

"The wisest mind has something yet to learn"
                    – George Santayana, Philosopher

High achievers realize that they are automatically going to be looked at as mentors because of their accomplishments and success. People want to pattern themselves after people who have a proven track record. Athletes are the best example of this. Every boy growing up, who wants to be a pro athlete desire to be just like the one he admires the most. This athlete represents the pinnacle of success for this young man. When I was growing up, I always dreamed of playing in the pro bowl. I knew that all the best football players in the world would play in the pro bowl every year. I could always see myself scoring a touchdown to win the game. I may not have made it to National Football League, but I am still a superstar. Every successful person is a superstar in their way. Make sure that the mentor you select considers you as a superstar. When your mentor appreciates your value, and understand your gifts, they will help you reach new platforms. Learn everything you can from those who mentor you.

Build A Stronger Relationship

You must develop an efficient relationship with your mentor. Your mentor will help you invest your finances and your time in the right places. Your mentor will serve as your quality control manager. They will help you make sure that you always put your best foot forward. I think all major corporations should partner experience staff members with new hires. This will help the new hires understand the culture of the company, as well as teach them how to achieve success in the corporate structure. It would create a healthy work environment that would reduce the stress level of employees. A mentoring relationship is forgeable in diverse places. Sometimes you find them by choice other times the circumstance that you find yourself in will dictate who that person will be. Never the less, build a strong and healthy relationship with them.

Mentors only want what is best for you. They will push you in places where you do not desire pushing. Your mentor is not worried about being your friend or telephone counselor. When we think about mentors, we think of a friend who has been successful instead of a coach who will kick us in the butt when we need it. There are some distinct differences between our mentor and our friends. I have listed a few examples for you to develop a clearer understanding of the role of your mentor.

Mentors	Friends
Will push you where it hurts	Will declare you have tried your best
Has more experience than you	Are known by your experiences
Teaches the difficult lessons	Sympathizes during the difficult times
Encourages more growth	Applauds you for what you have done
Challenges you to learn more	Is critical of your educational pursuits
Builds your capacity	Place their limitations on you

By having strong relationships with your mentors, they will help develop your raw talents. This is a significant point because you will soon find many people will become jealous of your new-found success. Your mentor must be a person who has proven that they do not mind helping people achieve more than even themselves desire to accomplish. It is imperative that the mentor understand his role as a motivator and inspiration. They must be an encouragement and not a hindrance to you. Everyone who claims they want to see you successful is not telling the truth. Beware there are some people out there who seem to be successful, but it is just smoke and mirrors. A real relationship with the person will take spending intimate time with them to learn their keys to success. Here are a few questions you should ask every potential mentor.

Mentor Checklist:

- What are you reading?

- Who has influenced you the most?

- Who is your mentor?

- How many people are your currently mentoring?

- What time do you wake up?

- Who do you admire?

Coaches Win Games

One of the greatest lessons I learned while playing sports as a child is that coaches win games. My football coach told me that players win games and that coaches lose them. At that time that rhetoric sounded very good. If you are a sports fan like me, you have heard many commentators utter those same ridiculous words. I have watched sports and mastered specific concepts of the sporting world over the years, and I have learned many truths. One truth that I learned is that I cannot play the game and pay attention to details all at the same time. Let's use the game of football as an example. Football is a game of inches. The game has become so sophisticated over the years that they keep adding the number of coaches that each team needs to have to be successful. They even have a booth for coaches now at the top of the stadium where a coordinator can communicate via a headset to the other coaches on the staff. These coaches are so important to the plays that are being called on the field, that they are paid very nice salaries. As a semi-pro football coach, I learned how crucial every decision I made was to the success of our team.

Coaches train their teams to be prepared for every possible situation that will present itself. They also teach their team to be mentally tough. Most coaches are effective managers of time and energy. They know how to put their players in the best possible circumstances. They give their players an opportunity to shine. A team with awesome talent and poor coaching will be a losing team more often than not.

We must remember two important things about coaches. First, most coaches are former players who were successful in their profession. Secondly, coaches are the masterminds behind the talented players in the games. Coaches use their players as chess pieces to successfully conquer their goals and opponents. We must also remember that when a team does poorly in the standings of their respective sport, it is usually the coach who gets fired at the end of the season.

If your mentor is not helping you create more wins in life, you should fire them too. They should put you in position to see the details more clearly. If your mentor helps you with the game plan all you must do is execute it with precision and you should see the desired results. Giving half the effort necessary will prove the pundit correct. You as player will be the reason you are not winning. Let your coach push you to the end of your abilities.

"In every man's life there lies latent energy. There is, however, a spark that, if kindled, will set the whole being

a fire, and he will become a human dynamo, capable of accomplishing almost anything to which he aspires."
— James Cash Penney, retailer

Motivation used right is a very effective tool in both life and business. If you want to accomplish more in life, you must be able to motivate the people around you. Family, friends, loved ones, and neighbors will all help you reach your goals in some way. Some of them will be team members others will be cheerleaders that help encourage you when times are rough. Motivation reminds me of what I learned about computers when I was a child. My dad told me if I put junk in I would get junk out. If you become a motivator of people, you will always be able to find a person who will motivate you.

A good mentor will motivate you as well. When they hold you accountable to your goals it should drive you to push harder. I have learned that the word try is unacceptable in life. None of my mentors would ever allow me to say I would try to accomplish anything. My wife tells me to eliminate all possibilities of doubt when dreaming and to discuss how we will reach our goals. Removing the words doubt and try from your vocabulary will really change the way you think and plan. This alone will motivate you to stretch yourself beyond your comfort zone.

**Leadership Alert:
"A mentor is someone who allows you to see the hope inside yourself"
-Oprah Winfrey**

"There is a powerful, driving force inside every human being that, once unleashed, can make any vision, dream, or desire a reality." - Tony Robbins

⑦ *Friend Or Foe?*

$\mathcal{H}$ere is one of the nuggets I hope you can grab hold of in a hurry. You are a business. Everyone has a business locked inside of them. You may not work on your business full time, but you have something inside of you that wants to get out. You may work in the factory nine hours a day and then come home and make gift baskets at night. That is ok if it fits your business plan. In today's economy you better have a plan A. Notice I did not say have a plan B. Your J-O-B is your plan B. You cannot rely on any benefits your job currently gives you to still be available to you next year or when you retire. The economy is changing every day, and so we must be prepared to handle those changes.

Sharpen your communication skills regularly. Every day you are being interviewed by society. You may not consider yourself to be a business, but you are conducting business unaware. One of the best jobs I ever had was presented to me while I was a manager of a shoe store. I was helping a client, and I gave what I consider my presidential service. The next day that customer called me and asked if I would think about working for the company she represented. Three days later I was meeting with the director of branch operations and going on a walk-thru of the corporate facilities. This would have never happened for me if I did not give this customer quality service. I did not know this fortune 500 company even existed let alone was hiring. Keep in mind that opportunity is always knocking at the door for you so prepare yourself to open the door.

The quality service I provided the customer opened doors for me that changed the rest of my life. There is nothing you can exchange for delivering five-star customer services. Every business should focus on customer service as a core competency. Stop reading this book thinking, but I am not a business. That is fine, but even individuals must provide quality customer service. We call this a positive attitude. You must become an agent of change. You should always have a positive attitude and a healthy outlook. Others should draw to you because of the positive energy resonating from you.

"Be a yardstick of quality. Some people aren't used to an environment where excellence is expected."
> - Steve Jobs, Apple Computer co-founder

I remember during my eleventh grade year of high school we had a substitute teacher one day in my marketing class. This teacher taught us that we needed to learn how to create our employment. I could not quite understand what he was saying, but that is because I was talking to the girls in the back of the class. I did pick up one thing from him though. He told us that the word job stands for just over broke. He taught us that our employer would pay us just enough to make sure that we would return the next day. I later learned that he was absolutely right. No matter how much I made on a job I always thought I deserved a raise. Even as a salesperson, I never thought I was earning my worth no matter how big of a paycheck I received. Many of you feel the same way I did. I began searching for a business that I could start that would give me an incredible earning potential.

We must look at our lives as a business. We can be highly successful in anything we do if we surround ourselves with successful people. Here is the difference between you and a major corporation. A major organization relies on quality people to make them successful, but give the people very little in return for their efforts. A company will use you until you are useless to them and then move on to the next person. As an individual, you should surround yourself with quality people, and in return, an exchange of wealth is created. Ask yourself this question will you ever make more money than the principal stockholder or owners of the company where you are employed? The answer is simple probably not.

Treat yourself as a business and enjoy the benefits of a corporate lifestyle. Let me crystal clear I did not tell anybody to quit their job, or to do anything unethical while at work. The lessons in this book are meant to stretch you to become successful wherever you are planted or desire to grow. If you are running a major corporation use my words to continue to grow in that position. For those of you who want to do something, unprecedented take the leap of faith.

Can I be a little technical at this point for just a moment? Robert Kiyosaki has taught those of us who have read his material about the cashflow quadrant. In his writings, he talks a lot about creating ways for money to work for you. Operating a business and investing our money are two avenues where we can make money even when we are not punching the time clock. I think it is essential for us to realize that there are many benefits to running a business. The most beneficial of these benefits is the tax write-offs that you will receive once you incorporate or organize your business entity. Employees taxes are different from those of a businesses. He also taught us that being self-employed is just as bad as being an employee. High achievers understand this and develop into smart investors or corporations. Many people are satisfied with just having an assumed name or LLC behind their name. Please do not allow yourself to get stuck in that place. Your original dream is much bigger than an assumed name. Remember you started with a humongous dream so that you could develop and achieve bigger things. Reach beyond small beginnings and become great. You must approach life knowing you are a business and that you will be successful despite the odds.

Invest in your business

Before you can hand in a resignation letter and jump onto the road of success, you better have the necessary credentials to survive. You must invest in yourself. You have to do the research required to find out what licenses if any you must obtain. What are the federal and local requirements to operate that type of business? Which business model is going to be the best one for you to use. Then you need to purchase books CDs and DVDs that will help you become successful. I recommend that you attend every workshop and seminar that you possibly can. Then visit websites of people that are doing what you do and see if your plan looks anything like theirs. I hope you get the point I am making. I had read so many books that when I moved into my new house, I had more boxes filled with books, tapes, CDs, DVDs, and notebooks than I did with clothes.

The most significant investment you make will not be your finances but your time. Reading requires you to invest time. Seminars require you to give up part of your day to listen to someone else tell you how to do things you already feel you know how to do. You should never feel like you know everything there is to know about any given subject. When you say you are starting a business, you are really saying I am finally going back to school. Yes, I said school. I hear you saying, but there will not be any professor to grade my papers or give me a surprise exam. On the contrary, there will be. Your banker will want to see your profit and loss statements. The electric company, gas company, and phone company know if you are successfully conducting business transactions every month if you pay your bills on time. Your customers will judge you on your prices or the quality of your services. There is always going to be someone watching to see how successful you really are. Preparation is only accomplished when a person is comfortable with the amount of effort they have put into a task.

Psychologists argue that the way a person dresses will determine their attitude toward success. My sister has always said that if you dress for success, you will feel like a success. When we talk about investing in ourselves, we must also consider our wardrobe. We must invest in clean suits, ties, blouses, slacks, and shoes. It is not about the name brand or amount of clothes that we own but the quality and the cleanliness of those clothes. People will hear the confidence in your voice when you feel like you are a success. The way you look will contribute to the way you feel on an everyday basis. You may not be able to buy a workbook or a CD today, but you can iron your shirt or press your blouse. Take that extra step and watch how others respond to you differently. Invest in every area of your life because your success depends upon it. I once heard a salesman say the very thing you cannot afford to pay for is the very thing you need to invest in now. He was right. If affording the training or necessary education to improve is difficult than you must invest in it to reach your desired results.

One word of caution that I would give you, however; is to become frugal in your investing. Do not become so hungry that you buy everything. Only buy things that you are going to have a use for in the near future. Every Speaker and guru has a product to sell. You must buy things that are going to add value to you. The objective of investing in yourself is to increase your value to the known world. It will also give you places to reference when you have questions and do not know whom to ask. Start with the recommended reading list in the back of this book if you are not sure what other books you should read, and keep an eye out for my next book.

Invest in confidence

"Confidence is the most important single factor in this game, and no matter how great your talent, there is only one way to obtain it-work."
– Jack Nicklaus, Golfer

The number one asset that you must guard with all your power is your confidence. Your confidence is more beneficial to you than you may realize. Once it is lost, it is the hardest commodity you will ever have to recover. It may be easier to erase the financial deficit of the US government then it will be to restore your self-confidence. Confidence is a building block every successful business, or high achiever must have. The definition of the word confidence is trust; reliance; applied to one's own abilities, or fortune; belief in one's own competency. High achievers understand and believe that one's own ability is essential to their future success.

How can you expect others to believe in you when you do not believe in yourself? Confidence is seen in a variety of ways including your dress, presentation, handshake, and promotional material to name a few. I remember being taught to look a person in their eyes and to shake their hand firmly. This tells the person who hand you are shaking that you have confidence in yourself.

Another principle my coach taught me was to walk fast and with my head up. This principle I learned did not work for my profession but was a perception that is widely held about confident business professionals. I believe you should walk with a moderate tempo with your head up and a smile. This tells others that you are excited and on your way to do something of value. You do not want to seem overconfident, arrogant, egotistical, or too busy to be approached. I have learned the hard way that when people think you are busy, they will not offer you new opportunities. Slow down and show people that you have time for them. After sitting in a workshop on building a referral pipeline, I change my voicemail greeting. My message now says, "I am not too busy for you, your family, friends, or anyone else that you would like to refer to me." This simple change to my greeting has produced more leads for me than I can count.

The harder you work on developing your character, moral attributes, and professional skillsets the more confident in your abilities you will become. Hard work on these things will ensure that others perception of you change as well. Your confidence is what helps set you apart from others in the mind of your clients, and competitors alike. Successful entrepreneurs know that they must build confidence in their product, service, systems and interpersonal skills daily.

There are several ways to build your confidence. Reading self-help and motivational material should be at the top of the list. These materials are full of great exercises and tips for personal enhancement. Tapes, videos, and CDs are great resources as well, that foster an environment for continued growth. Attend workshops and seminars that focus on personal development and self-help. Practice and rehearse your lines and scripts daily. I had one lady tell me that she did not need scripts because she was not in sales. I realized that when she made that statement, her business would never survive outside of her basement. If you are open for business, you are a sales representative first and foremost. How can you run a successful business or capture market share if your presence or product is not known? Practicing your scripts will allow you to relax more when you are talking with prospects. The more prepared you are, the more confident you will become. Earlier we discussed that you could ease tension and eliminate nervousness with sufficient practice and preparation. A person who is myopic in their thinking is a person who will not be confident in growing to their fullest potential.

Please remember that your confidence may be the first thing that others see about you. When I am done speaking, many people come up to me and comment on admiring the confidence that I showed on stage. They could see my confidence through my dress and posture before I ever opened my mouth. Everything about you must say confidence. Your confidence will help you eliminate any self-doubt that would try to speak to your subconscious mind.

The more prepared you are, the more confident you will become

"Experience tells you what to do; confidence allows you to do it"

– Stan Smith, Tennis Champion

My glass was half full

We have heard great teaching about perception. We all have discussed if the glass is half empty or half full. It took me a while to realize that my glass was half empty. I needed to pour more information in so that I could gain more knowledge. See when I say my glass was half empty I am not talking about my outlook on life I am referring to my knowledge of my industry. There was a lot I still had to learn about success and high achievement. I had to invest more time in practicing and developing my material. My outlook was great. I knew I had potential to be successful. I had all the tools to be successful but not all the information I needed. I think we often focus too much on perception and not enough on information. The more you learn, the stronger you will begin to feel. It is your inner strength that gives you the ability to have a healthy self-image and a positive perception. Now I would say that my glass is half full. My growth has equipped me with the keys to success, and I am learning how to walk with others as a high achiever in life and business.

When I was growing up I hated to read. I have a weird way of learning. I can sit through a speech and memorize it word for word get up and recite it without any practice just like the presenter. I did not learn how much of a problem this was for me until my son started learning how to read. He was four, and we were teaching him how to read Dr. Seuss. We read it to him every day and night. Well, when he entered kindergarten he had a unique quality that the teachers could not figure out. He could read a book to his teachers minutes after hearing the teachers read the book to him. He came home one day excited about this new book. I sat down on the bed beside him and he began to read to me. He made one little mistake though, he put the book down to put on his house shoe that fell to the floor- but he did not stop reading. Then I knew my son was just like me. He could remember whatever he heard someone say. Every book he had in his closet was recorded in his memory. My son was full of information but lacked skill.

Perception is just as important of a trait as confidence. What you perceive is what you believe. If you lack perception, you will either lack confidence or misplace it. You must remember that you are the product first. Your skills, talents, resources, and future products take a back seat to your personal development. As you develop your skills and stretch your capacity to build your business, it will become easier for you. Remember image is everything. Build your image, increase your self-worth, and stop cheating the process. When I learned the value of reading, I began to appreciate the work it required to become successful. I know believe I have both the skill and the knowledge to win in my field. My glass is full, and the overflow is helping those whom I mentor.

" A pessimist sees only the dark side of the clouds and mopes; a philosopher sees both sides, and shrugs; an optimist doesn't see the clouds at all – he's walking on them."

– Leonard Louis Levinson

⑧ *All Done By Noon*

*L*et's talk about your organization skills and your ability to prioritize. You will only accomplish what you are genuinely passionate about doing. I had a training session one day where I asked a young lady to describe where she would be in the next three years. I then asked her would she be willing to do it for free. She gave me the strangest look of all time. The reason why I asked this question is that whatever a person is passionate about is the only thing he is willing to do without pay. Passion is a concept that necessary because everyone will experience a learning curve and a down time in their business when they first begin. If you are not passionate about your business, you will give up midstream if you are not care-ful. You must have a deep sense of desire to do the little things that it takes to become successful. Greatness is a quality just as success is, however, to achieve greatness, you must pay attention to the minor details.

As I told you in a previous chapter, you need to make a list of five things that you must do for each day. Make every effort you can to do them in the morning. You must become programmed at this routine. You want to accomplish everything you can before noon. Make every phone call you can that will have a positive impact on your life and day. If you need to set a doctor appointment do it early in the morning, do not procrastinate. If you have dry cleaning to drop off do it early in the morning before class or work. One thing you will notice is that there will not be many people in line when you do things early. Go to the supermarket extra early before all the kids are there with their moms running through the stores. It is not that I do not like children. Children are just one extra body in the way at the store which makes the store more congested. Go work out in the gym while everyone who really needs to be there are still in the bed sleep. The idea of an early workout also demonstrates an earlier point I made about positive energy. When you go to the gym and work out before 7:30 am everyone there is serious about physical health. You will feel positive energy all around you. The sound of others on the treadmill, the bike, or the weight bench will put an impression on your mind not to give up on your goals of a well-balanced life.

Learn balance

It is vital that you learn to live a well-balanced life. You should live a life that has spiritual, emotional, and physical balance. Make it part of your daily routine to achieve these early in the morning. You will develop a sense of success by implementing this into your daily routine. Discipline yourself to focus on these three areas just as a major corporation would focus on customer service as its core value. A well-balanced person is a happy person. Happiness is underrated in our society now. We do not focus on making people happy anymore. When you live a happy life, you are more willing to face adversity head-on. You meet challenges at the doorway of achievement and defeat them.

Learn what I call the triangle of balance. If you are spiritually and emotionally balanced but do not take care of your health, you are still living a life that is out of balance. You will continue to struggle with pressure and stress every day you attempt to reach your goals, as long as you are not balanced. Balance is the key to unlocking your potential and positive energy. Let's take a closer look at the triangle of balance.

Wake up in the morning meditate and pray every day. Read something inspirational that will encourage you to become successful despite whatever odds you may be facing. Write yourself a note about the things you hear from your inner spirit in the morning. Be mindful it will take time to become comfortable understanding what that inner voice sounds like and from where it comes. Inner peace is born out of spiritual growth. Keep a journal next to your place of relaxation and then take it to bed with you at night. Journal the thoughts, dreams, and desires that come into your mind while you are at rest. Inner peace will cause you to have a laser-like focus on the tedious task you usually avoid.

Emotional Balance is just as important as spiritual balance. Make sure you develop a strong sense of self-esteem. You need to believe in yourself, your talents, and your gifts. You can have all the information in the world, but if you do not feel comfortable with your capabilities, it does not really matter. Learning to love, will help you achieve emotional balance. First, you must love yourself and then those closes to you. You should then establish some personal standards you want to achieve and reward yourself for success. When your emotions are in place, you will be able to handle the attitudes of others without hesitation. Criticism only comes to those who are active. The ability to manage criticism is a sign of emotional balance. The words of others will provide fuel instead angst when you are level-headed. Controlling your temper, passions, and past pains will separate you from those who live in a constant state of crisis.

Physical balance is the toughest for most people to obtain. This one takes you using some internal energy and effort. You must do something uncomfortable to get favorable results. Your diet is also important for you to have under proper control. Your diet will display your self-discipline. It will demonstrate your ability to control your desires and some unnecessary cravings. Your health will determine how positive you wake up in the morning. When you exercise in the morning followed by a proper diet, you will have more energy on a regular basis. Take vitamins to increase your energy. I realize the older I get, the harder it is for me to contain my weight. Exercise is a daily goal of mine. I attempt to maintain healthy habits.

Now let us review how this all works together. Start your day praying, meditating, reading, exercising, and eating adequately. Doing these things will cause you to feel better. Next, you begin to do your five must do's of the day and make all necessary phone calls before noon. You will be able to play hard in the evenings. I want you to realize that if you work hard during the day, you will get to play hard at night. Try this for a few weeks and track how much more you can accomplish in a day. I promise you will see great results which will even amaze you. I am not one of those experts who believe in all work and no play. I work hard to enjoy the finer things in life. Adjust your schedule to wake up before average people wake up. Finish your work as early in the day as you possibly can.

Time management

Successful business people are a great resource and time managers. They understand that these are two of their most significant assets. Most people are not in business but are employed by the business of busy/ness. You must learn to manage your time. See I have already told you to purchase a planner, but I must emphasize that it will not use itself. You must first put the information into the planner or calendar, but you must then hold yourself accountable to carry it out. Be mindful of the value of your time as well as others.

The average person does not understand how to read a profit and loss statement. Corporate America has taught them how much value they are worth per hour. People who think they are successful will tell you I make "X" amount of dollars per hour. This sounds successful to them, but this is far from what should be considered a success. First, how dare anyone tell me how much I am worth per hour? I refuse to allow someone else to tell me how much I am worth or what hours to work. Your boss or supervisor job requirement is to dictate to you how to manage your time.

I could care less what my worth per hour is. I am more concerned about what is my net worth. I am considered successful if my net worth increase regardless if I worked or not. By managing your time like high achievers, you will find yourself having free time while others are still at work punching the clock. The only clock I punch is my alarm clock when I wake so that it is already set for the next morning. I do not set my clock every night. I set the alarm in the morning after I am done using it. It is like when you tell your children to put something away when they are done using it so that they will know where it is next time they need it. I believe in using my time efficiently to ensure preparation for the task at hand. Time is money is what I have been taught as a child. I take that to mean if we do not waste money than we should not waste our time.

I avoid people who are time wasters. I avoid them because I know they are not high achievers or money makers. I want to enjoy the finer things that life has to offer me. I like to travel and wear nice suits. I enjoy eating at high-quality restaurants. Better yet I love doing these things while the average person is at work. I believe every day of my life should be an enjoyable one. You have no excuse for not being able to do many things in one day. Learn to be organized, prepared, and time sensitive. You need to learn how to tell time on your internal clock. This clock will always keep you focused.

The last thing I want to share with you about achieving greatness and time is those power producers are always early. To be on time is to be late. Setting your clock early to be on time is a poor method of time management. If you must do that you are really saying that you cannot trust yourself to be responsible. Successful people are responsible and time conscience.

Don't break the rules

It is essential at this point for you to begin thinking and acting as a top producer. High achievers know that they cannot break the rules. This is the foundational premise of their discipline. You must become like a broken record and do the same things over and over again. Do not lose focus of the little things while you are attempting to grow in success. Become an effective time and resource manager immediately. The pressure to succeed is less intimidating when you learn how to manage your time. Your friends and family will see that you are headed in a new direction before you even began to make any money. Success is a lifestyle, not a destination. You must apply these rules to every aspect of your life. You must also make sure that you do not allow other people to cause you to break the rules either. Do not let people put themselves on your schedule at times you have set aside for money-making or triangle of balance activities.

You have greatness inside of you. You can accomplish everything that you set your heart to do. It is time for you to dream big dreams and live life to the fullest. However, I must give you a word of caution here. Successful people always remember the things that made them successful. They remember to prioritize all their core activities. They are always researching information that may be important to their success. They create partnerships with others who are high achievers. They understand the importance of the triangle of balance. Keep yourself focus at all cost. You have many tools available at your fingertips now you must learn how to use them and become productive with them.

Make sure that as you begin to set your schedule for the coming week make sure to set time aside for personal development. Never let yourself become so busy that you forget to learn new things. It cannot be said enough that research is the critical component in developing into a successful dreamer. Dreams can only become a reality after you have learned as much as possible about a subject and carved out your desired niche. Make time to go to the library and bookstores. Take a class at your local community college or recreation center. It is important that you never lose focus on research and development. Many people think that once they begin to do the things they have dreamed of doing that there is no longer a need to learn. That is a myth. Learning should have a permanent place on your schedule.

"I made a resolve then that I was going to amount to something if I could. And no hours nor amount of labor nor amount of money would deter me from giving the best that there was in me."
– Col. Harland Sanders, Kentucky Fried Chicken Founder

Your passion will determine your effort. How much energy are you willing to invest in your future and your dreams? When I played football, we use to tell each other to leave it all on the field. Give it your best effort. It is up to you to reach your potential. You are the voice that can make your butt move. Speak life to yourself. Get rid of all your negative thoughts. Live the dream now. Your vision should be full of powerful energy so feed off it. It is time for you to realize that there is greatness inside of you. Let others begin to see how amazing you really are.

You have read this book and others long enough without moving into action. Write your goals and develop your game plan. Stop watching the game from the bench when you have been selected to be in the starting lineup. Nothing is stopping you from being great but you. Do not be a procrastinator but become a pro at what you do. You have opened your mind now open your heart for greatness. Believe that you are going to be a high achiever. See it. Speak it. Think it. Live it. Walk it.

Think Like It

It is time for you to be the best you can be. I know this is a phrase that the army used as a part of their marketing campaign but it is true. Real success starts with your thinking. I hope you have begun to realize the way you think will play a significant role in the amount of success you achieve. Stinking thinking will give birth to poor results. You do not have to settle for being second class or second best. You are not mediocre. Tell yourself that the sky is the limit for you. Let your thought pattern change. Renew and refresh your mind daily. Remove negative thoughts from your thinking. This will require that you get rid of all negative influences in your life. Negative people hang around negative people and not highly motivated people. You must guard your mind from the terror called negativity.

Start every day knowing that it will be the best day of the rest of your life. Look for something new to learn. There is always a nugget that can be found to make you stronger. You must remember that your competition is getting bigger, faster, stronger, and smarter every day. Each generation is further ahead than the one before it. In our modern times, you are not just competing with your generation, but you are also competing with the ones to come. Your job is in jeopardy if you do not learn something new today. Your business is closer to closing if you do not learn something new today. Your future is depending on the nuggets you learn today for success.

Learn to think you are successful. There are four power principles that you have learned in this book that will help you do that. Let us review them here; you must learn to think it. If you dream it, you can have it. You must learn to see it. Seeing is believing. You must learn to speak it. We learned from the book of life that there is the power of life and death in our tongue. You must learn to walk it. You can live in your dream once you have applied hard work and become passionate about being great. You must think like what you want if you are going to reach it. You must have contagious faith so others will invest in you. As you grow, you must impregnate others through mentoring and sharing your resources. Read like your life depends on it and then read some more if you want to improve. These principles will help you become successful.

Results happen over time. Success is like a muscle. You will put in long hours of work before you see consistent results. Do not take days off or sleep in late. Keep working even when you feel like giving up. Dark days will come, and frustrations will arise but do not let them overtake you. Continue to chase your dream. You are a dream chaser that one day will look back and smile at what you have accomplished. Life is a journey full of challenges and rewards. You may not control all the destinations, but you do control how you interpret them. Spend time today thinking about how you plan to move forward with the lessons you have learned in this book. Take your written notes and highlights from this book and write them in your journal. Meditated on at least one thing, you can apply from this book. If I have shared one thing that can help you move forward than reading this book was worth it.

Learn to change your perspective on things. The future is bright, and the best is yet to come. You have had set back and even felt lousy at times, but that is all over now. The power of positive thinking has taken over your life. You can achieve your dreams and become whatever you desire. You are a leader and not a follower. You are an agent of change. Today is a new beginning for you. Start dreaming, planning, and living the type of life you deserve. Work hard, play hard, love hard, and watch how it pays off for you in the end. You can be successful so

Think Like It.

Michael E. Carter Jr. – Recommended Reading List

Top Producers:

Tribes: We Need You to Lead Us Hardcover by Seth Godin - ISBN-13: 978-1591842330

Failing Forward: Turning Mistakes into Stepping Stones for Success Paperback by John C. Maxwell - ISBN-13: 978-0785288572

Leaders Eat Last: Why Some Teams Pull Together and Others Don't Paperback by Simon Sinek - ISBN-13: 978-1591848011

Eat That Frog!: 21 Great Ways to Stop Procrastinating and Get More Done in Less Time by Brian Tracy - ISBN-13: 978-1626569416

Designed to Lead: The Church and Leadership Development Hardcover – by Eric Geiger and Kevin Peck - ISBN-13: 978-1433690242

Winners:

Boundaries Updated and Expanded Edition: When to Say Yes, How to Say No To Take Control of Your Life Paperback by Henry Cloud and John Townsend - ISBN-13: 978-0310351801

The Go-Giver, Expanded Edition: A Little Story About a Powerful Business Idea by Bob Burg and John David Mann - ISBN-13: 978-1591848288

The 5 Levels of Leadership: Proven Steps to Maximize Your Potential Paperback by John C. Maxwell - ISBN-13: 978-1599953632

Communicating for a Change: Seven Keys to Irresistible Communication by Andy Stanley and Lane Jones - ISBN-13: 978-1590525142

Ageless Classics:

You Were Born Rich Paperback by Bob Proctor - ISBN-13: 978-0965626439

Think and Grow Rich by Napoleon Hill and Ben Holden-Crowther - ISBN-13: 978-1912032990

Rich Dad Poor Dad: What the Rich Teach Their Kids About Money That the Poor and Middle Class Do Not! by Robert T. Kiyosaki - ISBN-13: 978-1612680194

How to Win Friends & Influence People by Dale Carnegie - ISBN-13: 978-0671027032

Acknowledgements

This book would not be possible without the many people that stood by my side and help prepare me to walk in my purpose and destiny. We all have trials and tribulation but everyone does not have the type of support that I have been blessed with.

Family:

I thank my wife Tanika for her support, prayers, and understanding of the vision that I have for our family. Without her I would have given up on making this book a reality. I know that it was not easy dealing with me during this project. I want to thank our children for helping me put this book together and understanding why I could not give them as much time as I did before working on the manuscript. Your jokes and smile were encouragement that no one else could provide. Mom you are a rock that I could always count on and for that I say thank you. To my sister who always pushes me to check my data and know the facts from every angle I say thank you. It is because of her drive for perfection that I deliver quality presentations that touch the lives of many around the world.

Friends:

I am thankful to all of my friends who stood by my side during my time of writing this book. It is too many of you to name so I will not even try. You helped me push through the tough times that I have been through. I also want to thank all the rest of our team and partners for their support and understanding. This book would not have been published without the help of a few special friends.

Business:

I would like to thank the many mentors, coaches, and employers that I have had over the years. It is far too many of you to mention you all, but you all have played a major part in my personal development. Thank You for standing in my corner and teaching me how to develop my business. To the Champion Myles W. Miller who help push me to develop the right mindset your nudging paid off. To Edwin Channel for being the first person to believe in the vision and stuck with me as I went through the challenges of producing this project. Lastly, to all of my squad/tribe thank you for taking this journey with me and I look forward to seeing you at the top.

Think Like It

www.ingramcontent.com/pod-product-compliance
Lightning Source LLC
Chambersburg PA
CBHW020914090426
42736CB00008B/623